Angels Among Us
Messages From The Archangels
A Book of Channeled Messages

By

Kristy M. Ayala, M.A.

Published by: Kristy M. Ayala Press

Cover Design/Layout: Rudy Cortez
Photo Credits: All Pictures, Rudy Cortez

This book is intended to offer information, spiritual support, and comfort. It is in no way intended to be used as a substitute for medical care. If you are dealing with any medical, mental, or emotional disorder; please consult with your physician or therapist and use this book under their supervision. The author does not assume any responsibility for the improper use of this book.

ISBN: 978-0-578-09574-5

First Edition October 2011
Second Edition December 2013

Printed in the United States of America

~For God and the Loving Archangels~

Rudy, thank you for your unfailing love and support; not only during this project, but always.
I love you.

Doreen, thank you for holding a candle and lighting the path for me; your light is so bright. Thank you for your insight, knowledge, support, and integrity in all that you do. You have been such an amazing mentor to me. I love you.

My departed loved ones; thank you so much for your support and endless help through this important shift within my life;

I love you.

Team KMA; thank you for all of your love, support, and guidance every step of the way;
I love you.

~Contents~

Chapters and Page Numbers

~Preface~

As a young girl; I noticed that throughout my days, there were moments where information would move through me in such a way that in the beginning took me by surprise. Now, as an adult, I realize looking back that I was channeling information from a very young age. Sometimes, people in my life would ask me a question, and I would experience this tingling sensation that would begin at my crown chakra, and move throughout my entire body. I would open my mouth and information would move through me. In the beginning, it would take me by surprise, and often times it would take the adults in the room by surprise as well. I remember many scenes where people would seem to be "frozen" and staring at me after I shared the information that moved through me to whomever I was speaking. The information was sometimes "advanced" for my age and other times it wasn't necessarily advanced but rather, messages that were exactly right for that particular situation and said in such a way that seemed to bring healing and comfort. This was not something that I was "planning" so to speak nor was it information that I had researched and was holding onto just in case the right moment presented itself to me. No, it was divine intervention, messages that were being shared with others through me.

As the years passed; I noticed that I seemed to attract even more of these situations and they began to "spread" to people that I didn't actually know. People in a variety of places would look at me and start telling me very detailed information about their lives; in grocery stores, book stores, parties, etc. I became used to these experiences and found that the same channeling experience would happen each and every time. At the end of the conversation, no matter what the length, the person would always thank me for the comments that I shared with them, and then would say, "I'm not really sure why I told you all of that." Sometimes, they would also say, "I never really tell anyone about this." This became very much "normal" for me and my daily experience as I moved through my world.

I really enjoyed these experiences and found them to stay constant throughout my life; but it wasn't until I was an adult that

I really began to understand that I was experiencing something called channeling. I began to read about other people's channeling experiences, and found even more comfort and happiness to know that this beautiful experience was also moving through other people as well. Some of the other people; were authors and speakers whom I admired greatly for their beautiful contributions and insights.

I then began channeling messages for my clients in my monthly newsletter; and at this point I was consciously working with an ascended master, angels, or other groups to share messages of love and support. I enjoyed sharing these messages each month, and I began to receive guidance to compile a book of channeled messages. I was excited about the idea of the project, but kept it on the "back burner" for a little while; allowing it to simmer. Recently, I decided that it was the right time to channel this book which you are holding within your hands right now. The Archangels wanted to work with me to share their messages about a variety of issues and topics.

My intention in creating this book was to be able to share the messages that I received from the loving Archangels with you. I deeply respect my ability and opportunity to channel messages, and I took down each of the messages exactly as they came through to me. There was almost no editing within this book; only a few punctuation shifts and changes. All of the "editing" decisions were made by me first asking if I could make the changes and when I got a clear, "yes" I would add semi colons or commas etc. I truly believe my only job here was to be a scribe of the information that came through, so that you could receive the messages and support as the Archangels presented them to me.

I hope that this book will offer you insight, support, and guidance. I also hope that you will be able to feel the great amount of love and beauty that is woven into the pages and the words of this book. It is my humble honor to have been able to channel this book for you. Thank you.

~How To Use This Book~

I decided to include a "How To" portion here because there are a few ways that you can use this book. I encourage you to personalize and explore different ways to use this book to offer you support, insight, and comfort.

* You can of course read through the book, cover to cover and allow yourself to move through the messages in the exact order in which they are presented; at the rate that is right for you.

* You can also use this book as a way to receive "Daily Messages" for yourself.

You can hold the book within your hands and ask, either silently or out loud, "What is it that I need to know today?" or "What is my theme for today?" Then, while holding the book allow yourself to open the book to a page; the message on this page will be the message for you for that particular day. (The book will open to the "right" page for you as your energy will lead you through the law of attraction.)

* You can also ask a question about a specific issue within your life.

Again, holding the book within your hands, and asking either silently or out loud your question. Then, while holding the book allow yourself to open the book to a page; the message on this page will be the message for you for regarding your question. (The book will open to the "right" page for you as your energy will lead you through the law of attraction.)

* You can also use this book as a "reference" when you are working on a particular life issue; as each message has a title or theme. There are some Archangels who focus upon similar themes, so you can gain a breadth of insight and information about your area of interest or focus.

* I have included additional information, support, and activities in the appendix section of this book to support you in creating and fostering your own personal relationship with the angels.

Archangel Michael

Archangel Michael's name means "He who is like God."
Archangel Michael is a very powerful archangel who is here to
help eradicate fear from the planet. Archangel Michael is often
pictured wearing armor and carrying his flaming sword of light
which he uses to release fear based energy from people, physical
objects like buildings, and vehicles, as well as fear based thought
patterns. The Archangel Michaels energy is a royal purple and
you may be able to see sparkles or a purple colored aura while
working with him.

When I work with Archangel Michael; I can always feel a very
strong presence immediately come into the room. While I work
with Archangel Michael he stands to my right side. I do see him
wearing his armor as depicted in many artistic representations of
him; and I can see and feel the royal purple energy which is
associated with him. I find that his energy feels very much like
that of a strong and motivating honored teacher. I find him to be
very wise and supportive; I have found Archangel Michael very
easy to communicate with and very patient as well.

Life Purpose

"Everyone, all of you have a divine life purpose with which you are here to complete. This is a task, an assignment rather that you have chosen on your own. You have chosen this assignment because you felt very passionate and connected to this particular area or issue. You also knew that you wanted to make a difference in this area, so you chose to make it your life's work while you were here in this lifetime. I find that many of you feel unsure or uncertain about what your life's purpose really is. You have fears that you may not be doing what it is that you are here to do. Many of you are creating blocks to your work because you are afraid you may not complete the work accurately and this makes you freeze like a deer in headlights; due to this fear you do nothing. Or, you are spending time at work that is not satisfying to you because you feel or believe that you do not remember what it is you came to do.

You can work with me today, right now and I will help you to remember what it is that you are here to do. I will help to light that spark within you that has become dimmed by the many otherworldly distractions within your life. In truth, you do know what your life purpose is; it has always been in your heart. What is it that you have always wanted to do, take away all of the other outside circumstances and instead focus on your heart instead. There you will find your own personal truth as well as the answer to your question about your divine life purpose. Many of you know what this purpose is; however you hesitate daily to begin your work on this mission; you fear that you do not have what it takes to contribute; you feel that you are not ready and you tell yourselves, tomorrow, or when I have done this then I will begin my work. You have all that you need to begin to work on your life purpose mission right now today.

All that you need will be provided to you; all you have to do is ask. You are the only person who can fulfill your exact divine life purpose, only you. You are not alone in this task, you have legions of support with you; quietly awaiting your requests for support. I am also here with you ready to be a support system and a catalyst for you to begin this important work. Do not delay in this task, as it is very important. Heed the call of your heart and soul, it is time and you are ready dear one, you are ready."

Feeling Stuck

"This feeling of not knowing how to move forward is rooted in fear. You are afraid to make the wrong decision, many times I see you weighing all of your options and going over every detail, yet no forward movement is made in respect to your work. This is due to fear, some of these fears are fears of failure, while others are fears of success. Allow me to work with you so we can work together to release you from these binding feelings and fear based belief systems. We will work together to release that which is no longer serving you in a way that feels comfortable for you. This will help you in moving forward.

As people allow themselves to make the choice to move forward and take any type of action toward that goal, the feeling and experiences of being stuck begin to release from you. These are like ties or straps holding you back and your decisions are what allow you to cut through these bindings and allow you to feel free, and like your own self again. I will support you all along the way; you need not be afraid or believe that you must go through this alone. I am here to help and guide you on this path. Release yourself from these feelings today; it is not too late to experience feelings of peace, comfort, and forward movement in your life."

Finances

"There are some very misunderstood ideas and information about finances in your world as of now. There are some very big changes that you are experiencing as a planet surrounding these ideas of finances however. Many of you are experiencing them at this current time. Many of you believe that money is the source of your abundance and the key to your opportunities; however this is not true. God is the true source of all, including your abundance and prosperity. I see so many of you struggling with finances and with money. You work so very hard and center your days around this. You believe that this support is an external force that you must chase and sacrifice for. This is not true, rather by turning inward and asking for support from God you are able to open up to the divine flow of infinite abundance and prosperity.

You need not fight, or hurt to have this in your life, it is possible for you to experience a gentle and constant flow of prosperity. Many people are feeling the swift changes and impact in your world around money and finances right now and it is forcing people to readjust their understanding of its value and its place in your world. If you are feeling that there is a lack, a block, or problem for you in this area. It can be healed with a shift in your understanding of the universal principles of flow and abundance. Ask for support in this area and it will be provided to you; allow me to help you to release yourself from any entanglements in wrong thinking as it applies to your financial situation. This area as all areas can be healed if you are open to the healing."

Protection

"Protection is such an important aspect; and so many people are not using this as a means to support themselves in their busy lives. There are so many energies that are existing in your lives that are impacting your physical, emotional, mental, and spiritual selves. Many of you are not sure of how to use protection methods and that is why you are not participating in them while others of you feel that you may be inadvertently offending another person if you feel guided to use protection around them. In truth, this is not true, everyone benefits when shielding and protection methods are used. Just as you use protection and cautionary methods with your children; as should you use these same types of loving and supportive interactions with yourselves.

It is very simple to implement these shielding and protecting principles. I am able to support you as well to place an energetic screen or filter around you like a bubble of light which will help to keep negative or lower vibrating energy from impacting your precious body. Many times when you are experiencing feelings of sluggishness, lethargy, or listlessness it is due to the exposure of other energy that doesn't resonate with you. You feel these feelings and you aren't sure why. Over time these energies can build up and create dis-ease within the body and even create pain. It is very important to use some method of shielding each day. You can call upon me to use my shield of light to protect you from any and all harsh energies and I will stand by shielding, protecting, and cutting away anything that is not in your highest or best good."

Clearing

"Clearing yourself and your physical environs is a very important and critical lifestyle that should be embraced by all. You come into contact with so many toxins; whether they be negative or toxic thoughts, ideas, belief systems, lower energies, and earth bound spirits which you are constantly being inundated with this all day long. If you could envision yourselves as a sponge that has been used every day for as many years as you are alive, what would that sponge look like? Envision that sponge, how would it feel, and look? You can then imagine all that your precious body has been absorbing as well; as you move through your days.

Clearing is a simple but important tool that can help you to rid and release the debris that you are absorbing each day. It is important to do this clearing method often so that you can be in a state of your true self daily. There are many clearing methods that you can use; it is important for you to find the one or ones that you feel most aligned with. You can call upon me to help you with this clearing process; and I will help to cut away any attachments to fear, pain, or negative and lower thought forms.

You can also work with AA Raphael to help with this clearing process; as he can use his healing green liquid light to sooth you as he washes and clears away all that is not serving you. Nature is also a very powerful healer. Going out into nature and allowing yourself to connect with the trees, soil, sod, or sand will support you in this releasing and clearing process. Being in or near a body of water, whether that is the ocean, river, stream, or your bathtub can also support you in this process. If you are using the bathtub to participate in this releasing; remember to add some sea salt to the water as a way to fully release. The salt will actually extract lower energies from your body. You will notice a significant difference after participating in this or any clearing method. Many times you will feel as if a fog has lifted from you. Many times you will feel more like yourself again; less agitated, frustrated, or even less angry. When you notice that you are beginning to experience these negative types of expressions regularly; it may be due to the lower energies that you have absorbed; and not your true feelings or disposition at all.

If this is a new process for you; please ask me to support you in remembering to incorporate it into your normal daily life. Once you begin using this method you will realize the great benefits. It is so important to include this into your life; especially with all of the electromagnetic frequencies that you are also exposed to on a daily basis. Please remember that I am here to support you in all areas of your life, call upon me and I will be there, always."

Archangel Raphael

Archangel Raphael is the Archangel who oversees all aspects of healing and those who have a life purpose that involves healing in any way. This is a very large umbrella of healers which can include but is not limited to doctors and nurses, counselors, teachers, professional speakers, body workers, alternative practitioners, and many more. Archangel Raphael's name means "God Heals" or "God has Healed." When working with Archangel Raphael, you may feel a sense of compassion, support, and encouragement. Many people see the color green while working with Archangel Raphael as he is associated with this healing color. You may also feel a sense of calm and peace when working with him; as I have found his presence to be very calming.

In addition to supporting our physical health; Archangel Raphael also supports those who are already serving in a healing profession as well as those who would like to transition into a healing profession. Archangel Raphael wants to support all who have a divine life purpose that is connected to healing. If you are a healer and you want to work with Archangel Raphael; you can simply ask him to be with you to support and guide you with your work and career.

Healing

"Healing is a very important and complex process; one that everyone is working through in one way or another. I have watched through time as the understanding of healing has drastically shifted throughout the years, ages, and through cultures. You are now experiencing a radical shift and change from the lack of understanding in respect to healing that you have been exposed to over the last 100 years. Recently the idea of healing has been relegated to medicating an issue and not actually supporting the person in need of healing. This is not a complete or balanced approach to the service of healing. There is a large shift happening however; where the understanding of healing is being shifted back to include an entire vision of body mind and spirit, a more whole or complete understanding of this idea of healing. We are seeing a re-emergence of the old or ancient knowledge about healing and watching it being re-incorporated into your lives.

This fusion of healing that is being used is allowing you to truly begin to experience a healing, a true healing for your body mind and spirit. It is important to understand that healing can not only consist of one aspect of your lives; it must address all areas to support a full healing. We must not focus only upon the pain; but instead the reason the pain is showing itself in the body. All pain is coming or is rooted in another area, emotionally, spiritually, mentally; which after time of not being addressed begins to show itself physically. Know that you can experience a life without pain and hurting. I am encouraging people to seek out what has been thought to be an alternative support system or alternative therapies as a way to experience a complete health system. These treatments are not alternative; but actually ancient knowledge that has been used throughout time in many civilizations. They can be used to support you now; today. I would like to work with you and to support you in finding a practitioner or practitioners to help you find homeostasis for yourself; a balance, a resting place. If you would like to work with me in this area please ask me to support you and we will work together to find the right support system for you and for your family. When we begin to work together you will know that you have been connected to the right practitioners by the signs and signal that you receive from me. If you feel guided to get a second opinion; that is also a sign and support from me that there is someone else whom may be better suited for you.

Healing is a very multi-faceted issue; however it does not have to be filled with fear, sadness, or pain. In truth it is something that when balanced can allow you to experience a very multi-dimensional and multi-layered life full of joy and peace. Healing is possible, it is essential for everyone to find and support their healing process as a way to maintain personal balance. It is possible, take my hand and allow me to guide you along your personal journey toward healing today."

Healers

"If you are feeling called to do healing work; any kind of healing work I ask you to work with me so that I can smooth your path of healing. This is a very important life purpose and calling and I am happy to help and support you along the way. Those with a life purpose involving healing usually feel guided to help others at a very deep level. They tend to help others from the time they are very young; this type of helping behavior feels natural for these healers. Many times these children find that they are able to help others in many ways; and other people feel comforted, supported, and that they were in fact helped.

Many times healers can look back over their lives and remember many times when people would come to them for support. This becomes a constant for healers; many times these people are friends or family members; however often healers are approached by strangers who tell them very detailed information about them and ask for help in some way. These are all signs that you have a healers' life purpose. There are so many ways to heal; and the way to know which path is the right path for you is to trust in the divine guidance that you receive based on your natural interests and talents. If you are unsure of how to move forward with your healers path; I can gently guide you and together we can open the doors to your healing work.

A healers life purpose is very important indeed; as are all life purpose callings. Know that whether you are currently working in your healing profession now or not; you are still able to conduct your healing work on a daily basis. There are people, animals, plants, and environments that are in constant need of healing. You have the ability to make a large impact on your world right now; today. Be strong and confident in your natural healing talent; and ask me to help you release anything that could be standing in the way of moving forward of your healing work now. I am here to help you and to support you as you move through your days as a healer. You are not alone; there are many other healers as well. If you would like to be connected with other healers; I can support you in this; all you have to do is ask. I am able to help you in all facets of your healing work; and I want to help you today. When you have the resources that you need; you are able to help others more effectively. Partner with me on this journey and path of healing. Do not be afraid of this path; I will help you."

Counseling

"Do you feel guided to heal others through words, language, and information? Do you feel that you are already performing this type of healing support for your friends, family, and colleagues? Do you feel guided to help others to see the very best within them by supporting them through difficult issues in their lives? If so; you may be called into the healing work of counseling. There are many varieties of counseling that are available to help and support others while on this path. This is a very important and needed life purpose. There are many people who need the support of those who are truly called to do this work from a place of true support and service. Unlike those that are doing the work from a place of exhaustion or burn out or even more sadly a place of last resort. It is so important to be able to heal others by helping them to see through the fog that may be around them or within them. This is not a judgment upon them; however an opportunity to truly heal by shining a light into the fog or darkness and helping it to dissipate and gently guiding the person by the hand so they can see their way to clarity again. There are many avenues to this healing modality; if you would like guidance as to where your place is; please ask me to gently guide you and we will work together to create the road map that is right for your counseling healing profession and service.

For those that are already in this line of service and for those who are being called; it is of the upmost importance to remember to keep yourself balanced. It is very easy to allow yourself to constantly help and serve others while in this field; while simultaneously allowing yourself to go by the way side. This is not helpful to anyone. It is imperative that you apply the same level of care, concern, and support to yourself that you do for your clients. It is important to remember balance in your own life. Like a ball; perfectly round and able to move and flow easily; it is perfectly balanced at all times. Don't allow your life to become heavier in one area over another. This creates blocks for you and for your clients; even if you feel that you are dedicating the majority of your life to your clients' best interest.

You must understand that if you do not care for yourself with the same integrity that you do for another; you can truly not help or support them to the fullest potential that is within you. If you are not happy, balanced, or fulfilled how then can you offer any of those insights to your clients. This is of the upmost importance; I see so many counselors denying their own happiness and life experience in the name of service. I also see so many of you tired, exhausted and mal-nourished. If you are feeling that you would like more balance between work, rest, and play please ask me to help you. I will guide you to a complete and whole lifestyle where no one has to be excluded; not even you. You can be a better counselor when you fill yourself up first. I am here to support you in all aspects of your counseling work; including self care. Treat yourself in the same way that you would advise your clients. You are not alone."

Animals

"Animals are such loving and peaceful creatures; so many of us have had the opportunity to connect to these beautiful souls through our connection with our pets. This is a very special connection; one that can only be understood fully by those who have had a pet in the home in their own life. Pets are able to provide a great deal of healing, comfort, and joy to us in so many ways. They move into our lives at the exact right time to offer us what it is that we need to help us in our lives. We are also able to provide healing and support to our pet companions as well.

For those of you who are being called to do healing work with animals; this is an important calling indeed. Whether you are being called to work in a medical healing modality or by providing energy healing or even pet communication. This is a very much needed healing path. Those of you who are called to work with animals in some way feel a very deep and almost soul connection to animals. You can feel what it is that they want or need and you are able to connect with them almost instantaneously. Many of you have experienced a situation where animals begin to move toward you because they can feel that you understand them and they long to be near you. Many of you who are called into this work have a very gentle demeanor; very compassionate and loving.

If you would like to broaden your connection with animals as a way to work with them; allow me to show you the way. You need not be afraid of taking this gift and allowing yourself to help others to better understand and heal their pet companions. Not everyone is able to experience this deep connection with animals which you have. You have the ability to be a way shower and a connection between the animal and the human companion. If you are feeling that this could be something you would enjoy; please ask me to help you. We will work together to release any fears you may have about helping others in this way. This is an important life purpose, this is a healer's life purpose and I am here for you, now."

Archangel Jophiel

Archangel Jophiel's name means "Beauty of God" and is represented by a bright beautiful shade of pink. AA Jophiel's energy feels very light, bright, loving, and uplifting. Archangel Jophiel can help to uplift our energy and beautify our thoughts instantly. Whenever I work with her I instantly feel joyful and excited. I often call on her when I am going to be working with a client who is feeling sad or has heavy energy around them as AA Jophiel is able to infuse the space with very beautiful and positive energy very quickly.

I have also found that working with AA Jophiel is very motivating. Archangel Jophiel can support us in releasing that which is no longer serving us; including old items, clutter, and stagnant energy. Working with Archangel Jophiel to clear up and clear out the old is wonderful and can help us to make positive shifts very quickly.

Clearing The Clutter

"When you hold on to things that are no longer needed within your life; whether they be physical items, relationships, or beliefs they begin to become stale. Over time this old energy and this hanging on can create a heaviness within your home and your life. You see, once things are no longer being used, it is important to pass them on or to release them as a way to keep the energy of giving and receiving open. If you can imagine a two way street for a moment you will be able to easily understand what I mean. If one side of the street is constantly being blocked it creates distractions, difficulty, and frustration while simultaneously not allowing things to move freely. This too is true for your life experience when you hold on to the old. It is a must do to clear and clean out the clutter within your life. I know that at times it may feel overwhelming, especially if you have accumulated a lot of old "stuff" over the years. However, even working on one small project today will make a huge shift in the feeling and experiences you will have.

Cleaning out the clutter is like taking a huge heaviness out of a space and off of your shoulders, it will instantly lighten you and your surroundings. You will also notice that as you commit to clearing the cutter out of your life on a regular basis, your life will also begin to shift in positive ways. You will begin to feel lighter and in many cases you will be able to focus more clearly. As you simplify your life, you are better able to open up to the ebb and flow of the natural course of life. As you lighten and brighten your inner and outer world, so too does your experience of life begin to lighten and brighten.

The old closets, garages, attics, and basements that are holding dust, old boxes, and items which are no longer being used are actually creating blocks to the new experiences and energy which is trying to move into your world. I am happy to help you to move through this stuff and to release you from it. You don't need to feel bad about this, as this is an opportunity to make positive change. We will work on one thing at a time and you will see how wonderful it feels to let go of the old and to welcome in the new. Clearing the clutter is a wonderful way to step into a new place in your own life, and you need not wait another minute to begin this important task. Won't you please allow me to help you with this today?"

Moving and Shaking

"Moving your body is a wonderful way to clear your energy centers and to raise your vibration to a place of happiness and joy. There is no one way to move your body, it can be done through gentle exercise, dancing, and playing. In any way, that you feel guided to move and shift your energy is wonderful. I encourage you to play music in your home or while you are outside and allow yourself to move to the music; opening up your chakras and clearing your energy body. Laughing and having fun while you are moving your body also allows you to move into a place of happiness and joy.

Remember the joy you felt as a child running, playing, dancing, or even singing; not caring if you were able to master these skills, just simply enjoying them. This energy of pure fun and joy is a high vibration, one that helps to open you up to so much healing and so much light. This experience of moving and joy also helps to increase your ability to manifest and to clear away old energies that do not belong to you.

Allowing yourself to connect to the joy you felt as a child by laughing, playing, and having fun will also allow you to nurture, soothe, and comfort your own inner child. When you allow yourself to connect to your inner child, you are able to connect to joy, imagination, and youthfulness. This is an important energy for all to connect with regularly, yet so many do not take the time to do this. Playtime is very healthy and healing in many ways; and can create even more energy for you if you are feeling tired.

I would love to show you many ways to move and play today if you would like to call on me. I will take your hand and help to release any fears or feelings of discomfort about playing the way you once did. You see, that inner child is ever inside of you and once you connect, it will feel very natural. Take my hand, let's play and laugh today."

Appreciating You

"In your world of constant motion, and work you are bombarded with tasks, information and chatter throughout your days. I watch as so many of you continue to move through the motions of your days; one right after the other without taking any time for yourselves. You feel that you will take time for yourself on your day off or during a vacation or when you can. Yet, this day or time never seems to come for you. I watch as your energy becomes lowered from all of the stress and over work that you continue to embrace day in and day out. I watch as you quiet your mind and spirit which are pleading with you to do something to nurture and feed yourself. I see that you keep going, often forcing yourself to move forward, one foot in front of the other even when you are physically and emotionally exhausted. This style of living where there is never any time to stop and to breathe, to relax or to rest creates a great deal of static and pressure on you and your body. You see, you are so focused on the next step, the next task, the next accomplishment that you do not even allow yourself time to appreciate where you are or who you are for that matter. No, instead you focus upon what has not been finished or what must be done next; and this can create burn out.

You are not a machine; you are a part of the natural rhythms of life with all of the ebbs and flows that come with Mother Nature. Yet, you try to override these natural rhythms believing that they do not apply to you. However, this is not true; you see you must carve out time daily to appreciate you and to nurture yourself. When you allow yourself to continue on in this manner for too long, eventually your body and spirit will say enough is enough.

You can begin to shift this old unhealthy pattern today, even by making small changes in your lifestyle. Every little shift of time that you allow for yourself will create a huge reverberation allowing your body and soul a chance to be nurtured. It is important to acknowledge how much you do everyday rather than focus on how much you didn't do. It is necessary to do things that you enjoy doing purely for fun and enjoyment as a way to feed and nurture the soul. You must find ways and create the time to actually live your life and to appreciate the beauty that you bring to it. Focusing on "one day" is not the way to live, you must create the life you want to experience today; and this begins by making small changes now.

If you could see how wonderful and special you are; perhaps you would allow yourself the gift of honoring what you know you need and deserve every day. Making positive shifts to honor yourself does not mean that you will allow your responsibilities to be neglected, no quite the contrary. When you allow yourself the time and opportunity to do what you love daily you will have more time to accomplish your tasks and work; because you will feel replenished and renewed. I can support you in making these important changes and shifts within your life right now. Simply ask for my help and I will guide you gently toward a new way to live, one which is respectful and honoring of you."

Archangel Haniel

Archangel Haniel's name means "Grace of God" or "Glory of God" and she brings grace into our lives when working with her. Archangel Haniel is represented by the color Pale Blue, and her energy feels very kind, loving, graceful, beautiful, and supportive. When I work with her I always feel a kind of gentleness around her. I also feel her genuine comfort and guidance as well.

Working with Archangel Haniel can support you in many different ways in your own life. Archangel Haniel can support you in increasing your gifts of clairvoyance, supporting your sensitivity, helping you with your femininity and the connection to the moon and the moon's energies, to name only a few.

Grace

"When you are in a particular situation in your life where you feel that you would like guidance and support so you are able to step out into the world in a safe and comfortable way; whilst also bringing blessings, comfort, and support to others; you can call upon me to be beside you. Together we will work together to present this gentle and graceful part of you to the world in an easy and gentle manner.

Many times I see you experience stress or worries as you plan for your day especially as it connects to interacting and speaking with others at what you consider very important events in your life. Many times as you prepare for a large lecture or speech I notice these nervous energies around you. I am always available to support you in releasing these worries and to instead step into the energy of grace which will allow you to speak, think, and move in a more gentle yet powerful way. You will still be able to support others and do your work; however it will come from a more natural place inside of you. You will feel yourself move as if you are gliding and speaking as if the words are like beautiful music. You will experience a greater sense of connection to the experience as well, as you will become more relaxed and more able to step into the energy of grace.

While accepting grace into your life you will also notice that you feel more connected to your higher self as well. You will also notice that your life begins to move more easily and gently for you; as if you were floating. While in the presence of grace you are able to more clearly connect to your true nature. If you feel guided to work with me I am here for you always. You can simply ask me to be by your side and we will go to work together in any area of your life. You can also ask for me to support you in remembering to embrace the beauty of grace in your daily life; you need not wait for an "important" day to embrace grace. No, quite the contrary in fact you can embrace grace and a graceful life every day."

Clairvoyance

"You are all able to use and access your natural gifts of clairvoyance. They have been given to you all; and when you are ready to embrace these gifts I am here to support you in the process. Some of you are using these gifts regularly and feel comfortable in the messages that you are receiving. I can work with you to increase these gifts and to support you in understanding the messages as they come through for you.

Others of you may feel uncomfortable or nervous about accessing these natural and God given gifts. I can help you in releasing any fears about opening up to your gifts if you would like to work with me. We will work gently and at a pace that feels natural for you so that you are able to understand the gift that has been bestowed upon you.

Your gift of clairvoyance will allow you to see the messages that are coming through for you from heaven and to understand them. You will also be able to connect to your guardian angels and departed loved ones who are all supporting you as you move forward on your path. Learning to use your clairvoyance is like learning any new skill; however you will find that it is a very natural and beautiful process for you. I am happy to take you by the hand and to walk this pathway with you; both of us together. I am here to support and guide you; and I promise to help you as you embrace your natural gifts and understanding of spirit."

Moon

"I am very connected to the moon and her energies; as are you. Even if you are not yet aware of how you are impacted by the moons energies; I can support you in fully understanding and moving within the natural rhythms of her cycle. With each cycle of the moon we are given an opportunity to create, release, and receive divine support. This is the way of nature and this is the way of the moon cycle as well.

Many times when you are not consciously aware of the moon rhythms; you experience a change in your energy levels and mood. You may notice that you are feeling differently one day from the next; however you do not allow yourself the opportunity to move in rhythm with what your body needs and wants. You see your body is completely connected to the moon and understands that a gentle swaying or dance is taking place within her shifts and changes; thus taking place in your energies. It is imperative to allow yourself to embrace this dance and to give yourself the time, space, and compassion that is needed to move gracefully from one cycle to the next.

I see so many of you continuing to push yourselves past your limit on many occasions and for many reasons; and then you feel tired, exhausted, and disconnected from your true self. You become more like a machine then your true self. You need to allow yourself to slow down and to connect to your own inner knowing of what is right for you. You will actually have more time for yourself and your work if you learn to move with the dance rather than against it. I am here to support you in learning, understanding, and embracing this knowledge so that you can remain in balance within your life. I will work with you so that you can find a way to incorporate this ancient knowledge into your modern life; as it still applies to humanity today. I am here for you; please allow me to support you in this very important endeavor."

Archangel Ariel

Ariel's name means "The Lion or Lioness of God" this Archangel helps us to connect to the natural world for healing, information, and comfort. Archangel Ariel also supports those who have a life purpose involving environmental awareness, and activism. When I work with Archangel Ariel I immediately feel a strong and supportive energy with me. I often call upon Archangel Ariel for confidence and leadership support as well. Archangel Ariel is surrounded by a shade of pale pink.

When I think of the energy of a mother lioness; it reminds me of connecting to Archangel Ariel's energy; a strong, supportive, and also very loving energy. I feel that while working together I am better able to step into my daily activities with confidence and awareness. As someone who has always been conscious of environmental issues from a very young age; I feel very connected to nature and being outside. I have found that I am able to receive messages and support from Archangel Ariel while outside very easily as well.

Getting Outdoors

"Mother nature has an entire world which is available to you at any moment in which you choose to participate. It is a gift that is eagerly waiting to be opened over and over again. There are so many healing qualities within nature. In fact, you are indeed a part of nature; you too are connected to the seasons, the shifts, and the changes that are occurring all around you.

However; I see so many of you disconnected from nature and thus disconnected from yourselves. You spend so much time connected to electronic devices and you work inside under fluorescent lighting while neglecting your natural body clocks. You become out of touch with your own natural rhythms and then you experience a reduction within your personal energy. You see the outdoor world through windows but never connecting to it. You experience a feeling of lethargy, exhaustion, and even boredom. These are messages to you dear children that something is not right; something is out of balance.

It is imperative to connect to nature on a daily basis. Nature has an amazing way to heal you and to clear you from what is on your mind and from the stress you are experiencing in your day to day lives. Being in doors for long extended hours is not natural for you. It is also something that should be seen as a regular part of your life and not something that you do only on special occasions, such as vacation. No, it is a part of who you are and your spirit needs the connection as a way to keep you balanced. You don't need to spend a great deal of time or money to achieve this healing and balancing experience. Instead, even spending 15 minutes outside walking your dog, or sitting in your garden will help to bring you so much peace and insight. You are much more able to hear our voices as well. When you are able to remove yourself from all of the electronic frequencies and to quiet your mind; you will find that you are able to connect to your own spirit, and the energies of the natural world easily. It is all right there waiting for you.

Manifesting

"I hear so many of you speak about manifesting or rather creating what it is that you would like to experience within your lives. This is such an important gift that is right there inside of you. You have all been given this gift of manifestation which allows you to draw into your world that which you feel gravitated towards.

I see so many of you struggling and frustrated in so many ways in relationship to your physical needs. I can support you and help you to reconnect to this mighty and beautiful gift which is sitting inside of you right now. Even if you feel you have forgotten how to use it; allow me to reassure you that you haven't. In fact this is ancient knowledge that you hold and I can help you to reawaken and to reconnect to it now.

All you have to do is ask me to work with you and we will work together to create the experiences that you long for. You need not feel afraid of using this gift; as I promise you once we begin our work it will feel so very natural to you; as this is something that is as natural as all of life itself."

Connecting with Animals

"Animals are such amazing creatures upon this planet. In fact they are very wise and oh so connected to the natural rhythms of this planet. There are many of you who also feel this very strong pull and connection to the animal kingdom. You have felt it since you were very young indeed and it has been with you throughout your life. Those of you who feel this deep connection are called to continue your work with animals whether professionally or personally. Animals can teach us so much in their own way and we just need to allow ourselves to listen. There are also many of you who can heal animals with your natural healing gifts. Animals seem to find you; they can feel that you are connected to them in a unique way. Allow yourselves to acknowledge that this is a gift; you can hear the messages and the unique language of the animal kingdom; a language of love.

If you would like to increase your own personal connection to the animal world, simply ask for the animals to come into your life and they will. It is so important to allow yourself to recognize the animals who are already working with you. Do you take the time to notice the bird singing outside your window, or the little frogs in the pond as you walk by? These animals are all connecting with you and you can connect with them as well. Allow yourself to acknowledge them and you can even ask them what their message is for you. You will see, hear, feel or know the message when you allow yourself to open up to it. Animals are a gift, and you can gain so much by connecting to them."

Archangel Gabriel

Gabriel's name means "The strength of God" this Archangel brings many healing messages and important information to us while also supporting us in sharing the messages we have for the world as well. Archangel Gabriel is surrounded by a beautiful shade of copper.

When I work with Archangel Gabriel; I feel this beautiful and kind energy in combination with a great deal of strength and support. I feel a steady nudging and encouragement to continue to move forward with my goals and dreams. This Archangel also supports me in having confidence with the messages that I personally have to share with others.

Writing

"Those of you who feel compelled to write; you have felt this fire burning deep inside of you for a very long time. It may have been there with you throughout your life. This is a very important calling indeed, in fact this guidance or feeling that you have when you think about writing and publishing is a very clear message to you that this is a part of your life's purpose. You have something that is important for the world to hear and to know; and you are able to share it in the way that is unique to you.

Allow me to help you in releasing any fears that you may be experiencing about moving forward on this project. I am here to support you in creating this piece of writing into the physical form. I am here awaiting your request for support and guidance. I understand the feelings of fear or uncertainty that can arise as you approach the reality of this project; however it can move through you more easily if you allow me to support you.

Many times I see those who are writers become fearful of how to move forward with their book or writing projects. I see your minds begin to jump from one scenario to the other. I watch as the wheels within your mind begin to turn faster and faster as you wonder how you are going to find all of the support systems to publish and sell your work for you. I watch these thoughts and uncertainties contribute to your own uncertainty about your qualifications or abilities to contribute your ideas to the world in the written form. This is as you say, putting the cart before the horse.

Instead focusing on the actual process of writing will allow you to move your thoughts and messages from inside of you into the physical. As you make effort to move those words onto a page the energy supporting your writing project begins to build. I can support you in finding the other pieces of your project; we will work together as a team to birth your writing project into this world. You don't have to do this alone and you don't have to have all of the pieces sorted out before you begin to write. Allow yourself the opportunity to begin the process; you will feel the energy support you as you begin to move your messages through you. You will feel a calm and a release as these words and ideas transfer onto the page. You will notice that the feeling of tightness in your stomach and the longing to complete this very important project will begin to release as you move forward with this important calling.

Call upon me to support you in this endeavor; you have all that you need to be successful in this project. The feeling inside of you calling to you to write; will not dissipate it will only cry out to you more loudly until you write. I will support you every step of the way. Your messages are very important and I am here to support you in spreading those messages now."

Messenger

"Do you feel guided to help and support others through communication? I am here to support all of you who feel this passion to serve through speaking, writing, teaching, and counseling. This is a very important mission indeed and I am here to offer you support in any way that I can. I can offer you confidence and comfort as you move forward with your communication and messenger life purpose. It is a strong calling to speak and heal through messages.

You may notice as you look back over your life that you have been teaching or supporting others with words and language since you were a child. People would come to you and somehow you would know exactly how to say the right thing to support them. This is a gift that you have been given and it is one that will allow you to help many people who cross your path. I can support you in all of your communication and messenger work; whether that is personal or professional.

Many who work with me find that I am able to open doors for larger messenger platforms. I can support you in spreading your messages to many ears and those who will benefit from your messages. I also understand that the media is a strong and important platform which can allow you to reach people all around the globe who can benefit from your insight and support. I can help you to gain the confidence that you want to move into a larger platform including that of the media. I will support you in bringing opportunities that match you in a positive way as you move forward on your messenger path.

Those of you who are feeling unsure or confused about how to move forward on your messenger path; I can help you to gain the clarity and confidence needed to move forward. No matter what your current situation is at this time in your life; I can guide you and support you so that you are able to achieve and experience the dreams you have for yourself in regards to communication. I will support you and show you step by step information about how to move forward. I enjoy working with those of you who are eager and excited to move forward. I am here for you like a strong and caring coach cheering you on each and every step of the way!"

Children

"Do you feel a strong and deep connection to helping and serving children? I am here to support those of you who understand and can feel the connection to the little children of this planet. These beautiful little children need our support, guidance, and kindness so they are able to move forward and make their way in the world. These small little people are very wise and have a great understanding of what it is they are here to do. It is so important for us to continue to love them and support them so they are able to continue on their path with full faith and confidence all along the way.

There are so many of you who have a life's purpose involving helping children; this is a deep calling; one that pulls right upon your heart strings. You can feel and connect to children in a very special way; in a way many can not. In many ways you still understand how it feels to be a child and children have a natural attraction to you. They instantly like you and want to be around you; they can feel your deep understanding for them. I understand and respect this deep connection and I am here to support you as you continue with this very important work.

I see many of you feeling that the work that you are doing with children is not important; you feel that your contribution is not big enough. However; that is just not true; in fact you are making a huge contribution. The care, comfort, and support you are giving to your children and others will allow them to carry that forward throughout their entire lives. It allows them to then pass that same kindness and support to others in their world. Do you see how it ripples forward like the ripples in a creek? This is how large your contribution is; one that impacts many, many lives indeed.

Those of you who feel guided to work with children in a professional setting; I am here to gently guide you by the hand to support you in this endeavor. There are many ways to do this; look within your heart to find the way that feels most interesting and matched with you. You can find this connection by tuning into the things and interests in your own life; allow these to be a way shower to open the doors for the kind of work you can do with children. We need your support and love. You have a gift to share with these children. Your heart is so full of love and love is what these children need and desire right now. Together I can support you and open doors for you so you can find the perfect match and perfect assignment with children. I am here for you; just ask."

Archangel Sandalphon

Sandalphon's name means Brother or Brother Together; and this Archangel can support us in many ways including bringing our prayers to heaven and supporting our prayers being heard and answered. Archangel Sandalphon also helps those who are musically inclined to magnify their musical gift and to support musicians along their musical path. Archangel Sandalphon also supports families in connection with their children before they are born and letting them know the gender of their new child. Archangel Sandalphon has a turquoise aura color.

When I work with Archangel Sandalphon I feel a very gentle energy around me. I often work with this archangel when I am working with clients in my private practice. I play music during all of my sessions and I ask Archangel Sandalphon to support my clients in fully letting go and to open up to the healing energy of the music while we work together. I have found this technique to be very supportive of my clients over the years.

Healing with Music

"Music is a very healing and therapeutic modality to support you in all areas of your life. It can literally open you up to new and higher vibrations to support you and to lift you to a new place within your day and within your life. I see so many of you who understand the healing power of music; and you use it throughout your day. Some of you may not know or understand why you are so gravitated to playing music within your home or offices, and while you drive, but you know that it makes you happy. This is all that matters in truth, and this is the exact answer, it does make you happy, it can fill you with joy and joy is a powerful and magical energy to experience. Joy allows you to travel along the highest vibrations which connect you with your spirit and to loving energies. When you connect to a joyful energy you feel light, happy, exuberant, and free. This is a very healing experience, one that can support you in so many areas of your life.

When you connect to music, you allow yourself to connect to an invisible energy which propels you out of any heavy or hurtful energy. It allows you to actually raise your vibration and it also allows you to manifest your desires very quickly as well. Pay attention to times when you play music throughout your life; notice how you feel, notice if you are smiling and notice please the feelings within your heart. These feelings are the keys to experience healing through the power of music.

So often throughout time music has been used in celebration, as a way to support people to make work seem less daunting, to connect to source energy, for meditation, for ceremonies, and so much more. As you can see you can access the healing support of music in your life now as well. Do not allow yourself to miss this opportunity to connect to this beautiful gift which is here for you. You need not find one way to connect to music, there are infinite ways, enjoy finding the ways that you like, and embrace music today."

Connecting to Music

"Do you feel guided to play music or to learn more about the musical realm? I am here to support you in this endeavor dear child, simply ask me to help you and I will. There are so many benefits to connecting with and playing music. Do you feel guided to create sounds which create music to your ears and the ears of others? This desire that is within you right now is a gift; it is like a light that has been lit inside of you, one which will not die out.

If you feel called to create music and to connect to music I am here to support you in this endeavor. It is possible for you to move forward with your musical dreams and desires and I am here as a full and complete support system for you. All you need to do is simply ask for my help and we will work together as a team to bring your musical dreams and desires into fruition now.

What is it that you would like to experience with your music? Be very clear and very honest with yourself in regards to this matter; as I will help you gain the confidence and skill set that is needed for you to experience your musical dreams. I will bring people and opportunities to you to support you all along the way as well, and we will work as a unified team to continue to take steps forward at the rate that is comfortable for you. We can begin today dear sweet child, simply call upon me and I will be with you."

Connecting to Unborn Children

"As a new parent, so many thoughts and shifts begin to take place within your life as you begin to prepare for this role as a parent and this new addition to your life and your home. This change can bring about a lot of stress for some people as it is such a large life change. It is the beginning of a new chapter in so many ways for everyone who will be touched by this new life; however as a parent your life can seem to be impacted the most.

I am here to support you during this time of shift, change, and preparation. I can help you to connect to the spirit of your unborn child and to know if you will be parents to a little girl or a little boy. Many families find a great deal of comfort in this knowing as it allows them to begin to put things in order for the arrival of their new child. Many times this also allows the parent to begin to find a name that is suited for their child as well, names being so important; as they will carry the vibration and intention for the new child as they move through their world.

Many times I work with families during their dream time, allowing you to gain this important information if you choose to do so. All you have to do is ask me to support you in this way; and I will come to you. I can offer you comfort as you connect to your unborn child, we will do this together; I am here for you. You are not alone. There are many angels and family members in heaven supporting you as you prepare for this new life and new shift, we are here to support you, simply ask."

Archangel Jeremiel

Archangel Jeremiel's name means "Mercy of God" and this Archangel supports us in finding inspiration for ourselves and our lives. Archangel Jeremiel can also support us in remembering important dreams, increasing our natural clairvoyance, and also support us while experiencing a life review.

I have found that while working with Archangel Jeremiel he has a great deal of compassion and kindness that he extends with ease and grace. Archangel Jeremiel has a beautiful shade of dark purple which surrounds his aura, which I have also found to be very soothing and relaxing.

Life Review

"Dear children, there is no need to wait until the end of your physical life to experience a life review. A life review is a very healing experience, one that will allow you to see or watch the moments within your life. You will be able to connect with the moments you experienced again and to feel the feelings and understand the decisions that you made during each moment of your life. However, you will have the opportunity to see them from a third person perspective in a way, as you will be able to watch the moments unfolding before you own eyes. This is a very healing experience and an opportunity for you to understand why you chose one path over another.

I am here to support you in experiencing a life review now, today if you so choose. You need not wait; I can support you in this very beautiful process if you choose to participate. I will work with you to review an area or many areas of your life in which you may need additional support or guidance. We will work together to release any old beliefs, ways of working, or anything that you feel finished with as a way for you to move forward with grace and ease. This is an opportunity to shed old layers that you have finished with; and we will release them together one by one, allowing you to feel lighter and more focused. This life review experience is one that helps to open you up to a greater understanding of your own potential and ways to embrace your own best self. I am here to guide you through this process; simply call upon me and ask for my support and we will do this together."

Remembering Dreams

"We angels do much work with you during your dream time. We work together on all areas of your life. Many times you do not remember this work that we do upon your waking from sleep. The dreams that you experience are filled with important information which can support you in your physical life after you awake.

Many times you receive answers to questions or problems that you have been working on as well as messages of support, guidance, and insight. You may also connect to departed loved one's while dreaming, or even connect to the souls of unborn children. I can support you in increasing your ability to remember these messages and the work that we do together while you are in your dream time. I can support you in learning how to use the messages that you receive during dream time in your daily waking life.

One of the easiest ways to begin to remember your dreams is to keep a notebook and a pen near your bed each night. Upon waking, immediately write down what it is that you remember from your dreams as the information always applies to your waking life. You will begin to understand how the messages from your dream time can support you in your waking life as well. You can also work with me to increase your ability to remember your dreams upon waking. Allow me to help you to put the important pieces from your sleeping life together with your waking life. I am here for you, simply ask for my help."

Increasing Inspiration

"I see you; I see how wonderful and amazing you are in all aspects of your world and your life. I see how much potential and creativity you bring to your world each day. I want you to also see yourself in this way. I understand how your life can bring a great deal of tasks, stress, and constant motion for you. I watch how it can feel overwhelming to move through a day and feel as if you are not able to enjoy it in the way you want. I also see that over time this can contribute to feelings of sadness, or feelings of not being good enough. I see how damaging these feelings or experiences can be for you. I see how bright your light is which is shining deep within you right now; it radiates out to the world around you. However, these thoughts and feelings are like rubbing soot onto your light making it seem as if your light is not as bright as before. These thoughts can then lead you to experience feelings of stress, sadness, or even anxiety.

As you are able to release these feelings and thoughts it is like taking a cool washcloth and clearing and cleaning the soot away from your precious and beautiful light which is naturally bold and brightly shining. When you are able to connect to your own truth and your own light you will not be able to stop or diminish your own inspiring contributions in all areas of your life.

Allow me to help you to increase your own understanding and ability to get into touch with this beauty and passion that is sitting inside of you now dear sweet child. Allow me to help you to clear away the old beliefs, the old fears that are no longer supporting you. I will help you to reawaken your excitement for your life and for life itself. You are amazing and so full of light, allow me to show you."

Archangel Metatron

Archangel Metatron has a beautiful shade of lavender and green around his aura. Archangel Metatron can help us in many facets of our lives including better understanding and caring for sensitive children, clearing our energy, and understanding sacred geometry.

When working with this Archangel I immediately feel a great deal of strength and power. The powerful energy is very loving; however it feels very grand to me. I feel very safe and secure while working with Archangel Metatron and I also feel guided by him; similar to a relationship of a student and a wise mentor.

Understanding and Caring for Sensitive Children

"Dear children, you who are parents of the new and sensitive children who are on the planet as well as those of you who are preparing to greet your new children, please know that I am here to help you. You have a great and very important role as parents at this time in your planet's history. You are undergoing a great deal of social and political change. You are feeling changes in every facet of your life, global earth changes, social structure changes and on and on. All of these changes are making way for a new time and a new way that you will experience your world. As these intense and somewhat aggressive ways of life begin to shift and change for you and your world; you are now noticing an influx of sensitive children populating your planet.

These children are coming into your world at very high numbers and are continuing to come in on a constant basis. These children are here to help bring a more gentle and quiet approach to the new energies and experiences that are happening all around you right now. These children are very connected to spirit and they are clear about how to use their spiritual gifts; they remember where they have come from and they are not shy about speaking their truth. These children need conscious and loving parents to be stewards, and supporters for them while they are in your homes, classrooms, and even while on the playground. They need parents, educators, and support people to understand that their sensitivities to food, clothes, environment, and even noises are due to their fine tuned spiritual system.

Again these children are very clear, and they intuitively and physically know what is supportive for them and what is negative. Please listen to them when they tell you that something is not a good fit for them; as these children are very good at self soothing and recharging their batteries. It is important for these children to have a support system around them which will foster a complete and balanced approach to helping them as they move forward with the work they came here to do. If you need support along the way please work with me and I will lead you to kind, gentle, and supportive people to work with your children. I will also lead you to books, resources, and anything else that you may need to support your children.

Remember, you do have what it takes to be a steward and a positive way shower to these loving and sensitive children, and I am here as a support system to you. I understand that the parenting role is very important and that at times can be challenging; and I am here please call upon me to guide you and to offer you support as well. Remember parents that your children have chosen you to be with them along their path at this time and they know that you will be able to show them and lead them with love. Allow me to guide you and open the doorway for you and your children. I am here, you are not alone. Your children love you and you are loved."

Clearing Energy

"Loved ones; it is so very important for you to continually clear your energy as you move through your world. You have so many things that you are doing all at once; and so many of you never take the time to slow down or rejuvenate. In addition to this constant motion and lack of balance many of you are collecting so many energies throughout the day which do not belong to you at all. Some of them may be joyful energies, while others are sad, heavy, or even worry or anger filled energies. This takes a toll upon you this I promise, and if left unattended can contribute to feelings of sadness, lethargy, or even sluggishness.

These energies come from a variety of places and situations; including work, family, friends, and even fears you may be experiencing in your lives. From my vantage point I can physically see how this detracts and diminishes your precious energy and life force. It is like smearing soot upon a beautiful light bulb. The light is still there however it is much more difficult to see it or to feel the benefit of being near it. Allow me to work with you to clear your energy system of anything that you have collected throughout the day.

For those of you who are in very dense and heavy energy throughout your day please ask me to work with you frequently so you can maintain your high energy and stamina. For those who may not feel or believe that they are in any situations that could be draining your energy I also ask you to work with me as this is simply not true. You all absorb energy as a sponge picks up water. I will gladly conduct a gentle yet effective energy healing on you as a way to lift and clear these energies which will leave you feeling clear, supported, and fully restored to your natural self. This is such an important component of balance and regular health. However; I see so many of you not even understanding that this is needed as a way to maintain the quality of life that I believe you want to experience. I see you, I know that at your core you want to experience peace, happiness, joy, and love. I see you as a pure and loving being of God. Allow me to support you in keeping your energy high and bright."

Sacred Geometry

"Sacred Geometry is the make-up or foundation for all physical objects within your world. Each of these building blocks contains a vibration which is held within it; which allows it to vibrate at a certain level. These sacred geometric shapes can offer support and healing within your surroundings as well. These shapes can be used as a very powerful clearing and cleansing tool to clear away that which is no longer needed or no longer serving you. It can also be used to clear spaces within buildings, homes, or vehicles as well.

If you would like to work with sacred geometry or you feel guided to learn more about this healing spiritual topic then please call upon me to work with you. I can show you how to use sacred geometry for yourself and others. I can also help you by using this ancient and powerful knowledge as well. Sacred Geometry is like a key, a key which opens a great deal of insight, knowledge, and ways that have been used for thousands of years. Work with me; and I will show you and guide you."

Archangel Raziel

This Archangel's name means "Secrets of God." While working with this Archangel I always feel a great wisdom and strong leadership energy. I also get a strong sense of knowing that while working together I will be able to learn a great deal, as well as remember a great deal as also. I feel very comfortable and supported by this loving Archangel; and also very respectful of the great knowledge and understanding that I receive from him as well.

Archangel Raziel can help us to better understand our past lives and how past lives can impact us in our current lives. Archangel Raziel can also help us to better understand esoteric knowledge and spiritual truths; as well as increase our spiritual gifts. Archangel Raziel has a beautiful band of rainbow energy around him.

Past Lives

"Past lives whether you believe or understand the gravity of them; they are currently impacting your life today, right now. You can gain a great deal of knowledge and understanding about yourself, the work that you are doing, as well as the lessons you are learning within this lifetime by better understanding your past life issues.

By allowing yourself to connect to past life information you can actually release blocks, issues, or even fears which could be standing in your way of moving forward with more ease in your lives. This is not something to fear, no it is an opportunity to reconnect to the knowledge and wisdom which is sitting right inside of you right this very moment. Within your precious and wise body you hold all of the knowledge and memories from your previous lifetimes. Many times you tap into that knowledge by feeling an extreme fear of something that seems illogical or irrational to you in your life. By connecting to the root of this fear you will be able to gain more knowledge and information about why you feel afraid. In addition to this; you will also be able to reconnect to the wonderful and great knowledge that you have gained and collected throughout your souls' existence.

This connection is a beautiful experience; one which will allow you to better understand yourself in a multifaceted way. I would like to work with you to support you in better understanding your past lives and the contributions they are making in your current life. I would also like to support you in releasing that which you feel you are finished with as a way to support you in moving forward with ease, now. You need not worry about how to do this; I will support you and we will work together to make this healing occur in your life. Take my hand and we will do this together."

Understanding Spiritual Truths

"I see how interested and connected you feel to the inner working of the universe and God's perfect design. There are so many pieces so to speak which are right there available for all who would like to learn and understand more. I can help you to put these pieces together in a way which will provide a key to unlock these mysteries that so many before you were able to understand.

These spiritual truths or knowledge as you call them are available to everyone as they are existing, all of the time within your world, everyday. I will lead you to the information and I can support you in understanding how these spiritual truths impact you and your life right now. As you gain more information you are more easily able to make and experience the changes that you would like to see within your world. There are many resources available to you and I will gladly lead you to books, people, courses, and even memories which will continue to support your thirst for this knowledge.

Simply ask me to support you and I will. I will do a great deal of work with you during dream time as well; this way you are able to fully understand how the pieces of these puzzles fit together. I will also support you in remembering this information upon waking. Please work with me; I am here for you, ready to support you now, simply ask."

Increasing Your Spiritual Gifts

"You have all been given spiritual gifts, you have them inside of you right now. They are there, you simply need to learn how to use them in your everyday life. Many of you are aware of these gifts and you are ready and wanting to increase them. Using these natural God given gifts allows you to better understand yourself and the world around you. You are better able to move through your world making choices and participating in experiences which are a good fit for you. Your gifts can also increase your self esteem as you are then better able to truly connect to yourself when you are actively using them. I can support you in increasing these natural gifts; and also support you in releasing any fears with using them which may have come from negative messages or experiences from this or another lifetime.

Many times if you have experienced a negative outcome from using your spiritual gifts or showing interest in them; you can actually set them dormant. They are always there; however you need to turn them back on. I can support you in doing this. We will work together at the rate that is comfortable for you. Much work will be done during your dream time which is a time where you are rested and relaxed. Also dream time allows you to quiet your conscious mind; allowing you to be open to releasing fears about using your gifts. I will also support you in ways to increase the use and positive connection to your spiritual gifts while you are awake. I can pave the path for you to be led to the information and people who can support you in this endeavor. I will lead you to gentle, loving, and kind people; people who match you.

This gift of connection to your natural spiritual gifts will open you up and increase your positive energy, while also supporting you in all facets of your life. If you would like to begin down this path; I am here to guide you gently and respectfully. We will take one step at a time in the way that feels natural and supportive to you. Walk with me, I am here, simply call my name and ask for my assistance and I will be there. These are your natural gifts and you deserve to know how to use them, if you choose."

Archangel Azreal

Archangel Azreal's name means "whom God helps." Every time I work with this loving and calming archangel I always feel a great deal of support and courage. Archangel Azreal's energy is very soothing and supportive; like a kind and loving counselor; while also being strong at the same time. I always feel that I am able to have the courage to move forward while also feeling any emotions that are coming up for me while working with him.

Archangel Azreal helps us with endings and beginnings in our life as well as death and dying. Often referred to as the angel of death; Archangel Azreal offers support, guidance, and relief to all who are grieving and transitioning. Archangel Azreal provides a calming and loving support while also helping and guiding us forward. Archangel Azreal has a beautiful creamy white color around him.

Beginnings and Endings

"Beginnings and endings are a natural part of life. All things in your world are constantly shifting and changing, every moment. This is one of the main reasons that it is so important to value and appreciate each and every day as completely as you can, because change is all around you. You are a part of the natural cycles and ebbs and flows of life. For many of you change can be challenging; and you try to hold onto things tightly in your hands as not to feel the impact of change upon your lives. However, change is necessary. Change is the lifeblood that is pulsing through you, your lives, and all of the universe. You need change so you are able to move forward and experience new lessons and new opportunities. It is stagnation which is unnatural, not change.

Many times; I watch as you feel the sadness and grief as one door closes and another begins to open in your lives. It is natural to feel the emotions which come along with shifts and change as it is a new way of living, a new stage to experience. It is important to allow yourselves to feel and to remember all of the memories associated with what you are moving away from; but it is equally important to move forward with open arms and an open heart as well. To fear a change so much that you try to avoid it, can lead to more sadness and even feelings of anxiety. The more tightly you try to hold onto something which is finished; the more it slips through your finger tips.

You do not need to go through these transitions feeling alone or frightened. You are never alone, you are watched over carefully by so many loving angels and other beings of love and light who are helping you to move to the next chapter of your life; which brings new blessings to you. It is important to try and see the ending of one part of your life as the beginning of the next part of your life, a perfect cycle which is constantly moving you forward. If you feel uncomfortable or even fearful of changes, please know that you can ask me to be with you to comfort you and to help you better move through life's transitions. I can help you to see past the uncertainty and support you in moving through your grief and sadness. You live your lives moving forward, many times only to see or understand why the shifts and changes of your life are important after the pieces have begun to come together; you call this hindsight is 20/20. If you look back on the changes you have experienced thus far you will see how they have supported you and given you so much more than you ever could have know at the time; allow yourself to remember this as you approach the next bend in the road. Always hold on to the joys of your daily experiences as these moments are making up your life right now; they are yours, enjoy them."

Grieving and Healing A Broken Heart

"Grieving is not an easy thing to do, your heart actually experiences a great deal of hurt and pain; as you feel the sadness and even emptiness of your loss. The heart which feels all; aches for the love and connection from whom or what you have lost. It is so very important dear children to allow yourself to truly feel the feelings within your heart while you are grieving. Your heart knows what it wants and what it needs as a way to heal itself, and you. Your heart is a wise and knowledgeable "mind" of sorts. You can feel the tug or deep hurt that is moving through it; these are messages to you to allow yourself to feel these important feelings and to ride the waves of emotions like a beautiful sea. Holding your feelings inside or trying to ignore them will not work; you see they will continue to move through you, welling up giving you many chances to feel and heal over and over again.

There is no right time or right way to move through grief. So many of you feel the pressure of your very busy and overly scheduled world to hurry up and move on without taking the time that you need to truly feel and ride the waves that are moving through your heart center. You must find the way that is right for you to do this; and in the timeline that is right for you as well.

Many people do not understand that these waves of emotion move through you over the years, it is again constantly moving, shifting, changing, like you. There is no finite time line where the emotions stop, no, quite the opposite in fact. Again, when you feel this moving ocean move through you, allow yourself to move with it. Trying to stand still in these feelings or to push against the current is not easy it takes a great amount of work and effort, but to move with the current, this is the way to healing and peace.

In this time of your world with all things moving and changing so quickly, many of you do not take the time you need to receive support for your grief; you may not even know how to reach out for support. Know that I am here for you now and always. All you need to do is ask and I will be with you. We will work together to soothe your grieving heart and to heal the emotions or sadness which is moving through you. We will work together in a gentle yet powerful way and at the pace that is best and most supportive for you. You see, I can see into your heart. I know and understand your pain and how you are feeling. It is safe to talk to me I will help you each and every step of the way. You need not be afraid to tell me what is in your heart for you see I already know, and I am here to help lift the pain and hurt from you. I am here to help you heal and to gently support you in moving forward. I can even help you while you are sleeping which is a wonderful time for healing. Be not afraid, I am here for you, just ask."

Death and Dying

"Death is such a challenging time for so many of you. For those of you that are preparing to come home again, I see so many fearful for the end of their life; which is actually only the transition home. I understand this fear; and I can help to soothe your fears or anxieties about this transition. I am happy to work with you and allow you to see and to feel the love and beauty which is awaiting you. You see in truth your spirit remembers being home; it is always with you. You inherently remember the unconditional love and radiating beauty and joy that is waiting for you, and that is within you. However; it is easy to forget these feelings as you are exposed to the heaviness of your world.

You need not be fearful for the end of your life; as you are not alone. I am with you supporting you and guiding you home again. You will feel a lightness as you move closer to your loved ones who are waiting for you. Your memories of being home will rush back to you, and you will feel the experience of your saying, Coming Home. As you release your body, your spirit is free to soar and feels so much lighter and larger. It is almost like being able to breathe more fully; as you feel so free. You realize that you are not gone; your spirit is very much intact. You are simply moving out of the body which has served as your beloved home while you were in your life on Earth.

So many of you fear that you will not be able to be near or connected to your loved ones who are still living; however this is not true. You see, you are still able to connect with them as your love for one another keeps you connected to each other. You are still able to have a relationship with your loved ones as you are bonded together through love. Your loved ones hold you in their hearts and their minds.

I am here for you and for your loved ones who are grieving for your loss. I am here to support all of you in this important life changing transition. I can help to support you all in so many ways even in helping you to connect to one another. We can work together so that your communication can be understood by your loved ones; the signs, symbols, and hello's that you want to share with your family and friends. I am here to support you in this and so much more. I am right by your side patiently awaiting your request for help. Come with me, take my hand and we will heal and go home together."

Archangel Raguel

Archangel Raguel's name means "Friend of God" and this angel is represented by a very lovely light cool shade of blue. This loving angel can help us in all areas of our relationships and friendships. Archangel Raguel can helps support us in better understanding one another's point of view or bring healing to our relationships; whether they are personal, or professional. Archangel Raguel can also support us in bringing new and loving people into our lives as well.

I have found that working with Archangel Raguel is very helpful and very soothing. I feel that his aura color is so indicative of the way that it feels to work with him; I feel relaxed, supported, and I have even experienced a feeling of being "cooled" so to speak. I often bring Archangel Raguel into my sessions in my private practice as a way to better support both myself and my client. I find this to be especially helpful with new clients whom I have not met before; this helps them to release any nervousness or anxieties. I have found that Archangel Raguel has a calming effect upon my clients; easily allowing them to work with me in a relaxed and comfortable way.

Attracting New Friends

"As you grow, shift, and change, so too does your life; these changes also lead to shifts and changes in the people who are a part of your life as well. So many times I see that it is difficult for you to release or let go of the people in your life who are no longer a match so to say with your current life. I understand that this can be challenging for you; however like all things in life changes are always happening. Life is in constant motion; so too with your relationships. Some relationships that you will have in your life may stay with you for a long period of time, some even for a lifetime or many lifetimes. However; not all relationships are this way, no, in fact many are in your life to serve a purpose for a specific time and then these relationships transition out of your life just as they transitioned into your life.

It is important to be honest with how you are feeling about your relationships. Do your friendships and other personal relationships make you feel better about yourself or do they make you feel worse? Do you feel guided to avoid some people in your life or do you only see them out of obligation? If so, it is time to find a way to let these people move forward from your life. Holding onto relationships that have served their purpose does not support you and it does not serve the other person either. Holding on to finished relationships can actually create a heaviness in your energy level and create other kinds of blocks or challenges within your life.

I see so many of you hurting as you want to have new positive friends and relationships in your lives right now. You feel alone, and that you are not seen by the people in your world. I can see the pain that you experience by holding onto painful relationships. These feelings are not easy to feel yet there is something that you can do. When you let go of these finished relationships you make space for new people who are a better match to where you are in your life to come in to your world. I am here to help you in ushering in this shift within your life. I can see new people who are a better and more positive fit for you.

If you feel that you would like support in releasing the old and ushering in the new, please ask me to be with you. I am right here and I would like to help you clear away the pain and support you in preparing for the new. I can work with you to increase your beliefs about yourself and your standards so that you can better attract positive and loving relationships into your life. I can also help you to understand the life lessons that your former relationships provided to you and support you in learning these valuable lessons, so you won't need to repeat them again. I am right here; you are not alone."

Healing Old Relationships

"As you move through your life you will all experience some hurt, misunderstanding, or even more challenging feelings of betrayal within your relationships. This can be a very hurtful and heart aching experience for you. I see so many of you holding onto these old hurts and pains right inside your heart center. Over the years I see these old hurts become darker, heavier, and more cemented into you. I see the pain or resentments grow stronger and the sadness and even worse the numbness within you become a part of your daily life. This pain, though very real must be healed. Holding onto these heavy and toxic feelings are hurting you in so many ways. These feelings can keep you from experiencing positive and loving relationships in your life, including an honest and loving relationship with yourself. These toxic feelings can also create blocks to other areas of your life as well as physical and spiritual issues and problems. I can help you to release and to clear these heavy energies from your precious minds and bodies.

I see so many of you re-running tapes and re-exposing yourselves to the hurt over and over again. This adds more pain to your body and to your heart center. I can help you to heal from these experiences and to find a way to bring peace to yourself through the healing process. I will work with you at the pace that feels comfortable for you; never forcing you to move more quickly than you feel is right for you. However; I will push you in a loving way to be honest about what has happened and how you could have contributed to the pain as well as the other person. This is not about blame or who did what to whom, no not at all. Rather this is about releasing the hurts and learning from them which will allow you to move forward in a way that will support you in bringing more loving and kind people into your world. You will learn about your personal boundaries; and how to heal anything that could have in the past brought people into your life who were not respectful of your feelings. This work is about more than moving forward from the past; it is about healing and creating a better more loving future for yourself and all of the people you bring into your world. We will start with the fundamental relationship; the one you have with yourself.

You do not need to do this alone; or to feel fearful about what you have been holding onto. There is no judgment here. I only want to be of service to you; I am here to offer you my support, guidance, and comfort as we heal this together. I promise you that if you feel guided to work with me and ask for my support I will be right by your side. I will work with you in a way that feels natural and positive for you and we will clear your old hurts and pain together; you need not hold onto them a day longer. Today is a new day, I am right here for you; if you decide that today is your day, for a new beginning."

Harmony Within Existing Relationships

"As relationships are so important in your lives; it is also important to nurture them the way that you would nurture a beautiful garden. People and interactions with others are a natural part of your daily lives. It is wonderful and a gift to have friends and family who love you in your world. However; I have seen many times; relationships become strained or challenged due to a lack of care.

Most relationships which have been in your life for several years can begin to flounder if they are not treated with the same kind of care and love that they were given when they were new. In a way relationships are similar to owning a car. When you have a new car you are so excited to be with it and to use it. You want to keep it in the best condition possible and you talk to it and treat it as if it were they greatest friend to you in the world. Similar to the way most new friendships and romantic relationships begin as well. I see you going out of your way to support the other person, using kind language, and practicing random acts of kindness for the person as well. I see you thinking of ways to make the other person smile to reflect to them they beauty you see within them.

Over time however; I watch how these thoughtful and kind words begin to dwindle ever so slowly until they may become non-existent. I see so many of your relationships become cold or even routine. This is very sad and difficult to watch as these are the people in your world who you love and who love you as well. I sometimes even watch as these fundamental relationships become a source of sadness for all people involved. I watch as the light that was once so bright within the relationship becomes dimmed because the people involved no longer take the time to see the other person. Many times the communication falls away from the relationships as well. This can lead to feelings of disconnect, sadness, and even boredom.

There are so many things that can be done to support your existing relationships and to nurture them back to a place of beauty again. Like a beautiful garden, you must nurture all of your relationships if you want them to continue to bloom and to nurture you. I can support you in bringing your relationships back to a place that feels new and exciting again. Many times a lot of the work begins first with you. When you feel good about yourself you are able to begin to share these feelings with the people in your world. I can help you to experience this and to shift your relationships back into a place that you desire them to be again. You are not alone in your feelings of dissatisfaction. Your partners and friends would also like to experience the fresh and life affirming feelings in the relationship as well. I will guide you through messages and gut feelings about changes that you can make to begin to heal and awaken the love and excitement that is still within your relationships. Simply ask me to support you in this very important endeavor and I will be with you immediately."

Archangel Zadkiel

Archeangel Zadkiels' name means, "The Righteousness of God" This loving Archangel who has an aura which is a deep indigo blue color helps those who feel guided to teach, as well as those who are students or who want to maintain a razor sharp memory. Archangel Zadkiel can also support us in healing former memories which may have caused us hurts or pain.

Whenever I have worked with Archangel Zadkiel I have felt a great deal of support and encouragement. I have always felt that he has been a strong support system for me in many ways but especially before I do any public speaking or teaching.

Teaching and Leadership

"So many of you are born to lead and to teach; I see that it is part of your life's purpose and a part of your soul. You have been teaching since you were small children; this gift has always moved through you as easily as breathing. However, many of you feel uncomfortable bringing your ideas or insights to others in any formal way. I see how many of you dream of participating in teaching classes, workshops, or even leading small groups within your homes; yet you stop yourself from moving forward. I see how it hurts your heart when you choose not to allow yourself to move forward with this important life mission. Many of you doubt that you have what it takes or that you are fully prepared to teach another. I see that when you have this deep calling within you to teach, then it is time to begin movement toward this goal. If you feel fearful of public speaking, I can help you to release yourself from this fear and to support you in becoming more comfortable with your speaking abilities.

Many of you also fear that you will not find anyone to attend your classes or workshops; I can support you in finding a topic and students who will be a good fit for you and your knowledge. You need not focus on all of the things that can be a problem, but rather focus your attention on what you can contribute and how you would like to contribute. This will support you in moving forward toward your dreams of teaching and leading. There are many, many people who would love to learn more about the topics you are passionate about. You need not wait until some elusive time to begin your teaching and leading work, you can begin right now. I am here and I can support you in so many ways. All you need to do is ask for me to be with you and I will communicate with you through gut feelings, insights, and also messages that you may see. We will work together to find the ways that are most comfortable for you to work and to teach others. There are infinite ways to teach and to lead, we will work together to find your way; simply ask."

Students

"I love to work with students, both professional students and those of you who consider yourselves students of life. I can help you increase your ability to remember and to recall information easily. While working together I can help you to keep your mind and thoughts clear of clutter and other "things" that you do not need interrupting your learning process.

I can support you while in the classroom environment so that you can better understand the information which is being taught to you. Many times the instructor may have a different communication or teaching style than you are used to; I can support you in taking the information in and to see it in a way which makes sense to you. I can also support you in finding teachers and courses which are a good fit for your style of learning.

There are so many wonderful things to learn here; and I can support you in increasing your interest for learning something new while also support you in mastering what you are currently learning. I love to learn and I love being able to help others truly enjoy learning as well. Many times when frustration sets in while learning something new; it may be because you haven't had a great deal of exposure to this area or interest. I can work with you to help you see this subject or interest in a new light as a way to support it connecting for you.

I would also like to work with you to give you more confidence in yourself in relationship to learning. You see many of you tell yourselves that you are too old to learn or too old to return to formal education. This is simply not true, not true at all. Everyone has the ability to learn and to grow, and age does not impede this truth. If you would like to have more confidence and support to go back to school; I would love to help you with this area. I can also help you to receive support from those in your family as well. You see, I watch as you encourage those around you but all the while holding your own support or encouragement back from yourself. I can help you to believe in your own abilities and potential so that you are better able to believe in yourself. We can do this together; you see you are never alone. If you are feeling that you want to accomplish something; but you are holding onto the fear that you will not be able to accomplish your dreams; please allow me to help you. I see that the sadness which you hold in your heart about not finishing something; and this is much more challenging to you than you realize. You can finish what you have started or begin something new; I am right here and I would like to be of service to you now."

Healing from the Past

"I can see your heart and into your memories. Your memories are like a scrap book of moments, moments in time which you hold close to your heart and your mind. These moments which you choose to be so close to, create your beliefs and impact the way that you move through your world each day. You see, the happy and joyful memories contribute to your overall feelings of joy about your day and your life. When you hold many of these memories close to your heart and within your mind, you look for joy in other areas of your life, more photos to add to your scrap book. When you hold tightly to the difficult and challenging memories you also experience the same outcome. You begin to feel those memories and think about challenging thoughts throughout your day; and begin to notice or feel similar feelings as you move through your days as well.

Everyone has experienced challenges within their life; so much can be learned from these situations. In fact, you have moved forward to where you are at this moment because of the experiences that you have has so far in your life. However, I can see how holding onto the most challenging memories and moments of your lives and reliving them throughout your days can be very troubling for you. I can see your heavy hearts and heavy minds; I can feel the sadness and even confusion about why you have experienced what you have in your lives. I can see you creating very large walls and boundaries to keep others from coming too close to you and your heart, for fear of experiencing any further hurts. However, what you do not see dear children, is that these borders that you create actually keep you from experiencing the most happiness and joy which is available to you. You see, you are cutting yourself off from experiencing your own life fully. I do understand and feel the pain and sadness that you are feeling and I do understand why you feel it necessary to self protect. However, I have another alternative for you. I can support you in releasing the heaviness that you are feeling and I can help you to heal those old moments and to begin to move forward. I can work with you to heal the memories from your past which can help you to build bridges over the old boundaries and borders as you will no longer need them.

The memories, lessons, and insights that you have learned along the path of your life will always be with you; oh yes, however I can help you to heal and begin to create a new life; one where you are better able to bring positive and loving experiences to you. I promise you that the releasing of the old hurts and anger will feel like huge weights have been lifted from your heart and your mind. You will be able to feel like you can breathe more fully and live more freely as well. I have also seen people physically look and feel younger as they release the old heaviness which they have kept under lock and key for so long. I am here for you, and if you would like my help I would love to work with you so we can heal your heart and mind together."

Archangel Chamuel

Archangel Chamuel's name means "He Who See's God," and this loving and gentle archangel has a beautiful light green or peridot color around him. Archangel Chamuel can help all of us to see more clearly and at a vantage point which can allow us to see the bigger picture within our own lives. Archangel Chamuel can help us to find or see many things or issues within our lives in a better way; allowing us to also better understand our path.

When working with this loving archangel, I have found the experience very rewarding and very healing. Arhcangels Chamuel's energy feels so light and gentle and he has helped me to gain clearer insight into so many areas within my own life.

Finding Missing Objects

"I am here to support you in finding what you are seeking. You see; I am able to see what it is that you are looking for; and I can help you in finding it as well. For instance, when you have lost something and you feel that you have looked in every possible place; yet with no positive results; please ask for my help. You see, I am able to locate your item immediately and I will also lead you to it.

We will work together and I will guide you to the correct location of your misplaced item. Pay attention to thoughts and feelings that you have when you ask me to help you find what it is you are looking for. Many times, you may think, "but I have already looked there." Please just follow the thoughts and gentle nudging that I give to you as this will allow you to locate your lost items. Many times you may even physically feel me move your body very gently in the correct direction of your item as a way to show you that "this is the way" to finding what it is that you have lost.

I can also support you in this way if you are lost while driving or while looking for something in a store that you are not familiar with. Simply ask me to help you find what it is that you need and then pay close attention to the ideas, feelings, and nudging that you receive from me. By working with me in this way; not only will you find what you are looking for, but you will also increase your understanding of your innate spiritual gifts. Please know that I am here, awaiting your requests for help."

Finding Life Passion

"In addition to helping you find lost objects; I also help those who are searching for their life passion. So many of you feel frustrated or unsure of your life's passion or your life purpose; however I can see where your path is leading you and why. You see all of your life experience, lessons, and relationships create your life experiences and all of these create a pathway for you. Upon this pathway which is your life you have endless opportunities to make choices and experience different outcomes. With these choices, your natural desires, tendencies, joy, and passions are perfectly interwoven. Your natural tastes and dispositions outline your natural life passions and life purpose.

I see so many of you struggle so much to understand this simple but important truth which is already sitting within you right at this minute. You need not look outside of yourself to understand what your life purpose is; you see it is already inside of you now. Your natural attractions and talents point you toward the direction of your life purpose or your life passion. I can support you in making your life passions more clear for you. I want to take your hand and support you in bringing the right people and opportunities onto your path so you can enjoy and help others through your natural talents and gifts.

You need not be fearful that you do not have what it takes to make a difference in your world or to fulfill your life's work. You see, you are the only person who can fulfill your life's work and you are the only person who can do this in the way that you can do it. You see, your path is uniquely yours, and yours alone. Your contributions and your talents are equally important and supportive as others contributions. If you would like to work with me; I would love to support you in moving forward with your purpose. I will help you to better understand your path and how you can move forward while also supporting you in releasing fears and doubts. You can do this; and I am here to support you today and always."

Seeing The Bigger Picture

"Sometimes your life may feel that it is moving in a direction that may feel challenging or confusing to you. You have made concrete plans that seem to go awry, or you try to move forward yet you feel as if blocks are put upon your path. All of these experiences, although very real for you are all happening as a support system for you. This may seem unclear at times; and I can also see that these experiences can also cause real hurt and pain. During these times, you may feel alone and I want to reassure you that you are never alone. You are fully supported always.

In fact; I am able to see from a larger vantage point than you may be able to during times of distress or frustration. I am able to see how what appears to be a block is actually creating a better opportunity for you or allowing divine timing to support you at the right moment. I am able to see how the building blocks of your life are being constructed in answer to your prayers, intentions, and visualizations.

I would love to help you to better understand and to see this for yourself. I would love to work with you during your dream time and during meditation. I will take you by the hand and we will look at each life area which you would like more understanding or where you would like to see the bigger picture; and I will support you in releasing the fear that you aren't being helped or supported. I can help you to better understand why some things are moving at one speed and others are happening at another speed. I can help you to better understand divine timing and how it applies to your life and your projects. Being able to see from a new perspective can bring a great deal of peace and comfort to you. I would like to help you and all you need to do is ask."

Archangel Uriel

Archangel Uriel's name means "The Light of God" and has a gentle creamy yellow color around him. Working with him; I have found that I am able to be gently guided toward the information and answers to my questions. Archangel Uriel has a very kind, supportive, and loving energy which comes through as being very soothing and gentle.

You can work with Archangel Uriel to help you find what it is you may be looking for in any life area. Archangel Uriel is often pictured holding a lamp as he helps us to find our way. I love this image of the lamp because his energy looks like a warm candle light which always makes me think of shedding light onto situations; and illuminating new ideas.

Finding What You Are Looking For

"Throughout your lifetime, you will look for many things; including career, relationships, answers, homes, and many more things. In truth, all of the answers and information is already inside of you, you see you hold your own lamp of truth within you at all times. However, at any time that you feel lost or that you would like some additional support in finding what it is that you are seeking I am here to help you.

I hold my light and shine it upon you and your path illuminating all which is around you now. I can help to show you that it is safe to move forward on your path and also that you are not alone, not now and not ever. I can help to shine the light on the answers and support that will help support you as you continue down your pathway of your lifetime.

Many times; when you feel stress or worry it may become challenging for you to see clearly. I am here to help clear away some of these doubts and fears and to remind you that all is well and that you are safe. You will feel my warm and calming energy around you when you work with me and I will help to gently guide you out of the darkness and into the light. I will help you to reconnect to your own light and your own truth now."

Life's Work

"Your life work and your current work may not necessarily be one in the same at this time. If this is so, and you are feeling that you would like to realign your work with your life's work, I can help you in accomplishing this goal. You may be feeling a tugging at your heart asking you to begin to move into your personal calling, the work that you are passionate about. Many times; I watch as you feel fear and insecurities about how you will move toward your life's work. Many times you may not fully understand what it means to truly practice your life's work. I can help you and guide you to a better understanding of this very important yearning from your heart.

In truth, you have always known what it is that you were meant to work on while you were here. Allow yourself to connect to your passions and desires within your heart and your mind now. What images do you see? How do you feel? You see the calling or life's work is always with you, it sits inside of your heart space reminding you that you have what it takes to breathe life into this work, simply by being alive. You may need additional training or support to provide your gifts of service to others; but you have the ability to move forward today.

Part of your life's work may not be work that you are paid for; this I see can sometimes be confusing for some. You can always move into work which you are financially compensated for which is aligned with your life's work, of course, however some of your life's work comes from a place that allows you to serve in a day to day way which may not lead to a financial exchange.

I can help you to better understand your life's work if you are feeling unsure of its nature as well as guide you to the next steps along that path. I can support you in walking through the doors that will bring the right people and resources to you; supporting you all along the way. You need not do anything alone; and I am here."

Lighting Your Lamp Of Peace

"Inside of you all, you have a peace and contentment which can not be distinguished or tarnished in any way. Yet many of you feel that you have lost your way or your connection to your own light. You may have allowed outside hurts or relationships to make you feel separated from your own light.

However; I assure you that your light is burning brightly within you now. Allow me to show you and help to reconnect you to your personal truth and beauty. We will work together to release the residue and old hurts which could have been keeping you from noticing your own bright light of love and truth. Your light is equally bright as the light of others. When you are able to connect to your personal light of love, peace, and truth you will be better able to shine your light upon your path and the path of others as well.

If you are feeling lost or in a dark space, you need not look outside of yourself for answers, but instead turn inward and connect to your light. When you foster your light of peace and love, you allow it to burn brighter and stronger which fuels great love and inspiration within you. These components of love allow you to move forward in a strong and gentle way. Take my hand, let us work together to reconnect to your light of peace today."

Archangel Nathaniel

AA Nathaniel's name means "Gift of God" and has a reddish and warm brown tone around him. When I work with AA Nathaniel I feel a strong and forward motion energy; it is almost stern in a way. AA Nathaniel's energy is very loving and supportive but it also feels very no nonsense and "let's get the job done" at the same time.

AA Nathaniel helps us in moving forward on our path and supports us in releasing that which is no longer serving us so we can move full speed ahead on our projects and work. AA Nathaniel supports us in moving forward on our life purpose; and encourages us to take action now.

Let's Go, The Time Is Now

"Let's go, it is time to get going on what it is that you have come here to do. You will not be able to move forward by sitting on the couch, brooding, or focusing on all that is preventing you from moving forward. Instead, focus on what can be done, and begin to make those changes now. You see, the longer that you wait to begin your work, the heavier and stronger the pull is to begin. You may feel stress, worries or even anxiety because you are avoiding your natural calling. Once you begin to move forward on your path, these feelings begin to lessen for you and your life begins to come together more easily for you.

You need not try to do this alone. You see all the worries about how and when keep you frozen in fears and doubts. These energies do not allow you to see the potential and possibilities that are available to you because you are focused primarily on all that can and will prevent you from your dreams and true work.

Allow me to be a support system for you. I am here and awaiting your request for help. Asking me to support you will allow us to blow open the doors on your life and begin to clean up and clear out all that is no longer working for you; including these poor me thoughts and belief systems. You will need to be willing to do the work and to make the guided human action steps, but I will help you all along the way. You will not be alone I will be there supporting you as we go together through these positive changes that will support you and your life. There is no need to wait any longer, I am here and the time is now."

Life Purpose

"Your life purpose is not some illusive thing or a carrot on a string, no it is the longing and joy filled space that is already within you. You see, you already know what it is that you are supposed to be working on; it is releasing the fears that are crippling you from moving forward that is necessary here. It is ok to ask for help to make the changes needed to begin this path. You don't need to feel alone, and frightened like you are sitting in a darkened room all alone. There are so many who can help you and God works through people; people who are in you world right now, and those who will come across your path.

However, first you need to make the first steps toward what it is that you know is right for you. What do you love? What makes your heart sing? What is keeping you from moving forward in the direction of these passions? What do you believe needs to change or shift to make these passions more prevalent within your life? Do you know others who are working on similar projects or areas with which you are interested? Asking for help always opens doors; I would much like to help you if you would only ask. You see; I am able to see from a larger vantage point than you; and I am able to help you move toward the direction of your dreams. We can move forward together, hand in hand. You simply need to ask for my help and I am there. I can help you to release the old bonds of fear that may have been keeping you chained to the past. We will let go of all of the old as a way to welcome in the new. Won't you take my hand today?"

Fears

"Fears although helpful at times to keep you safe from dangerous activities and other harmful experiences are for the most part serving as barriers to your dreams. It is important to acknowledge the fears that you have and also to begin to move through those fears. It is in moving through the fears that you are better able to heal and learn. Fears can feel crippling and even scary at times, yet allowing yourself to step into those fears and through the other side allows you to experience a greater understanding of what is possible for you. You are better able to see a clearer vision of yourself and of the infinite possibilities which are available to you. Your world becomes larger, and more rich; and you are able to picture or visualize yourself in scenarios that you may have once never believed to be possible for yourself. As you are able to see or believe this bigger picture for yourself you are better able to experience this bigger life. You are also better able to release the fears that were crippling you in the past. As you release one fear, it is easier to move through more; each like old chains or shackles being thrown away allowing you to go from walking slowly into a full run. You will feel much more light and free; you will be able to connect to the child like joy and love that is naturally inside of you, the joy that tells you that life is full of love and possibilities, the one that tells you that you are full of love and possibilities. Be not afraid of your own power and possibilities. You are fully supported in all areas of your life, and you are never alone."

~Appendix~
Working With The Archangels

I have included a list of some of the "main" areas of focus for each of the Archangels that I included in this book. I hope that this chart will help you as you continue to work with the Archangels.

Michael

* Safety and Protection
* Releasing Fears and Moving Forward
* Protection of Service Professionals
* Life Purpose and Soul's Contract
* Fixing Mechanical and Electrical Objects

Raphael

* Healing You or Animals
* Supporting Your Healing Career
* Supporting Safe Traveling
* Connecting You With Soul Mate Relationship

Jophiel

* Organizing and Reducing Clutter
* Beautifying Our Thoughts and Beliefs
* Space Clearing

Haniel

* Clairvoyance
* Moon Cycles
* Healing For Women

Working With The Archangels

Ariel

* Connecting With Nature
* Manifestation
* Environmentalism
* Careers Supporting Mother Nature and The Animal Kingdom

Gabriel

* Supports Messengers (Educators, Writers, Musicians, Actors)
* Delivers Important Messages
* Supports All Aspects Of Parenting

Sandalphon

* Support For Musicians
* Healing With Sound
* Delivering And Receiving Prayers To and From God

Jeremiel

* Life Review
* Clairvoyance
* Understanding Spiritual Gifts

Metatron

* Supporting Sensitive Individuals
* Sacred Geometry
* Understanding Esoteric Knowledge and Insights

~Appendix~
Working With The Archangels

Raziel

* Remembering and Healing From Past Lives
* Esoteric Knowledge and Wisdom

Azreal

* Supporting Spirits To Return Home
* Helping Those Who Are Grieving
* Supporting Grief Counselors

Raguel

* Attracting New Friends
* Creates Harmony Within Relationships
* Healing To Misunderstandings

Zadkiel

* Students
* Healing From The Past
* Educators

Chamuel

* Finding What You Are Seeking
* Experiencing Peace
* Greater Understanding, Seeing The Bigger Picture

Uriel

* Students
* Understanding Information
* Excelling in School

~Appendix~
<u>Working With The Archangels</u>

Nathaniel

* Move Forward Rapidly
* Release The Old
* Take Responsibility And Guided Action Steps Forward on Life Path

~Appendix~
<u>Connecting With The Angels</u>

There are many ways that you can connect with the angels. By connecting and communicating with the angels, you can begin to nurture your own personal relationship with them in a way that feels good to you. Connecting with the angels can also allow you to create ways to work with them on areas within your life where you may want some help or support. Your angels will always respond to your efforts to connect with them. You may receive your "angel response" in the form of feelings, visions, thoughts, or a knowing after connecting with the angels. You may also receive signs such as; birds, butterflies, angels shaped cloud formations, angel feathers, or even rainbows as messages letting you know that the angels have heard you and they are with you. I have included a few methods on how to connect with the angels here; however I also encourage you to create your own ways to connect as well.

Angel Letters

> You can connect to your angels by writing them a letter either by hand or on the computer. Simply create a quiet space within your home or office where you won't be disturbed. You may even want to turn off your cell phone so you can really settle into your letter writing process. Then, simply begin your letter to the angels in a similar way that you would begin a letter to a friend. You can even write: "Dear Angels," at the top of the page. Then, allow yourself to write openly and honestly about how you are feeling and what areas you would like support, insight, and help from the angels. Allowing yourself to "free write" will really allow you to get your true feelings, thoughts, and emotions out into the letter which will allow the angels to have full access to the areas within your life where you would like help. Remember, the angels respect

~Appendix~
<u>Connecting With The Angels</u>

our law of free will, so we must first ask for their help so that we may receive their support and intervention. After you have finished your angel letter, you can either put it into a special box you may have as a way to turn it over to the angels, you can burn it in a safe and well ventilated area, you can bury it in the soil, or you can create another way to "hand" the letter over to your angels.

Getting Outside In Nature

This method is a wonderful way to open up to your angels; as getting outside into nature is a great way to clear and to quiet your mind. When we are in a place of stillness, quiet, and peace we are better able to hear the angels. Many times when we are rushing about

during our daily routines, we have so much going on that we can actually "tune" out the messages that we are receiving. However, when we make time to get out into nature we can actually slow down, breathe deeply and open up to the messages, support, and insight the angels have for us. We can also allow ourselves to better receive this support; as we are in a more natural state. Once you have allowed yourself to relax and to quiet your mind, simply ask the angels any questions that you may have for them on any life area. Then pay attention to the thoughts, feelings, visions, and messages that you receive. You can continue to ask questions or simply "talk" with the angels for as long as you feel guided. You may want to bring a small notebook with you so you can write down the messages that you receive; which will allow you to reflect back on them later.

~Appendix~
Connecting With The Angels

Dreams

The angels can work with us at great lengths during our dream time. You can even ask the angels to help you while you are sleeping. I would recommend having a notebook and a pen next to your bed for this method. As you are preparing to go to sleep, you can simply ask the angels to work with you while you are sleeping; and to help you to remember your dreams when you wake up in the morning. There is no "one" way to ask for their help, you can either think your request, you can ask it out loud, or you could even write it in an angel letter. During your dream time you may have dreams of working or talking with the angels. The angels can help you with any issues or questions that you may have; and they can offer you solutions, ideas, support, and guidance during your dream time. Many times, people will also receive healing and clearing from the angels while they are sleeping. Upon waking the next morning; before you get up to begin your normal daily routine, write down everything you can remember from your dreams. These notes that you write down will have important information and support for you from the angels. You can use this method at any time; however you can also choose to use this method for several evenings in a row. By choosing to work with the angels during your dream time for several nights or even for a few weeks you will begin to see common threads of support or messages that really stand out to you; offering you specific insights and support.

~Appendix~
Affirmations

Affirmations are a wonderful way to strengthen your confidence and ability to work with the angels. Affirmations can help to shift your thoughts and beliefs by using positive statements and feelings. You can use the affirmations below as a support system in working with the angels. You can also create your own affirmations to tailor make a support statement based on your own personal needs and desires.

There are many ways that you can use affirmations:

* You can write them down on pieces of paper and put them up on your bathroom mirror and read them while you are getting ready in the morning.

* You can record the affirmations you feel connected with and then listen to them on your MP3 player throughout the day.

* You can print out a "fancy" copy of your favorite affirmations and frame them and keep them on your desk or somewhere else that you spend a lot of time, so you can reflect upon them throughout the day.

* You can read them into a mirror, and watch yourself affirming what it is that you want to experience within your life. (You can do this at work or at home)

* You can create your own special way to work with your affirmations, as there are infinite ways to incorporate affirmations into your daily life.

~Appendix~
<u>Affirmations</u>

* I easily connect with the angels daily.

* I love to connect with the angels.

* I feel comfortable working with the angels.

* I feel safe working with the angels.

* I know that I can work with the angels at any time I choose.

* I am a highly visual person.

* I can see the angels auras and shapes clearly.

* I am open and receptive to the angels guidance and support.

* I am easily able to hear my angels messages for me.

* The sounds of the angels are something that I enjoy.

* I am open to hearing the messages my angels have for me.

* I am a very sound oriented person.

~Appendix~
<u>Affirmations</u>

* I understand the feelings that I have when working with the angels.

* I am very connected to my feelings, and understand them perfectly.

* I am a very feeling oriented person.

* I understand the ideas and thoughts that I receive when working with the angels.

* I feel comfortable connecting with the information, knowledge, and insights that I receive when working with the angels.

* I am a very thinking oriented person.

~Appendix~
<u>Meditations</u>

Below you will find some meditations that can help you to work with the archangels on a variety of issues, areas, and topics. Please feel free to create your own meditations, or to add any other areas of focus to the meditations that I have included here. I hope that you will enjoy using these meditations as a way to focus your attention or "work" with the archangels. My intention is that they will help to build bridges of communication, support, and love between you and the loving archangels.

Archangel Michael

Thank you for helping me to clear and release everything that is no longer serving me. Thank you for helping me to set down old burdens, fears, and ways of living that no longer match me or my life's purpose. Thank you for giving me confidence, clarity, courage, and the support to make forward motion toward the direction of my dreams, now.

Archangel Raphael

Thank you for helping me to heal, release, and soothe any heaviness and old pain that I may be holding within my precious body or my mind. Thank you, for supporting me in letting go, forgiving, and opening up to love again. I know that by focusing on love; I am able to begin to heal and to move forward in all areas of my life. Thank you for staying by my side and healing me with your gentle loving and supportive energy.

~Appendix~
Meditations

Archangel Jophiel

Thank you for beautifying my thoughts, feelings, surroundings, and physical environment. I know that when I feel good; I am able to spread joy and love to all areas of my life. Thank you for continuing to support me in infusing high vibrating energy, thoughts, joy, and love into all that I think and do.

Archangel Haniel

Thank you for shining your gentle grace, dignity, and beauty upon me today and always. Thank you for supporting me and encouraging me to step into my own best self and to move, think, and speak with grace and beauty today and always. Thank you for supporting me in opening up to my own natural sensitivities and for helping me to honor my natural gift of spiritual sight.

Archangel Ariel

Thank you for helping me to get outside into nature where I can better connect with you and all of the angels. Thank you for supporting me in opening up to the magic and healing of nature and all of her inhabitants. Thank you for supporting me in remembering how to use my natural gifts and talents in relationship to manifestation. Thank you for helping me to open to door to the magical realm and to connect to this wonderful world filled with joy, happiness, and peace.

~Appendix~
<u>Meditations</u>

Archangel Gabriel

Thank you for guiding me to the right people, places, and opportunities to spread my messages. I know that as an angel who focuses on supporting artists, writers, and other communicators you can support me in moving forward with my divine life purpose in relationship to spreading messages of love and peace. Thank you for guiding me to the exact right places and for giving me confidence and support as I share my messages today.

Archangel Sandalphon

Thank you for supporting me through the healing power of music. Thank you for leading me to the music, sounds, and sound therapies which will allow me to let go of the old and step into the new. Thank you for reminding me that music allows me to raise my vibration, and to clear my mind, body, and spirit. Thank you for supporting my prayers, affirmations, and positive intentions; as I know that you serve as a bridge between the physical and the spiritual.

Archangel Jeremiel

Thank you for helping my heart to heal from old hurts and to be willing to forgive and to move forward. Thank you for helping me to evaluate and to take "stock" of my life thus far, and to let go of old habits, ways of living, or beliefs which are no longer serving me. I know that I am fully supported in starting fresh and can easily find new healthy ways to deal with stress or old hurts.

~Appendix~
<u>Meditations</u>

Archangel Metatron

Thank you for helping me or my children in relationship to sensitivities. Thank you for helping me to better understand the sensitivities that I and or my children possess, so that I can better support, nurture, and embrace these gifts, allowing them to prosper and grow. Thank you for leading me to educators, health practitioners, and other support people who will understand these sensitivities and who will serve as a support system to myself and my children.

Archangel Raziel

Thank you for helping me to understand and remember any past life issues which could be related to my current life issues. Thank you for supporting me in releasing and healing any old: hurts, pain, or relationships that could have a past life connection for me right now. Thank you for helping me to heal and to let go of the past; and allowing me to gain any insights or knowledge and then moving forward with ease and grace.

Archangel Azreal

Thank you for helping my heart to heal from any grief, sadness, hurt, or pain in relationship to endings and beginning within my life. Thank you for leading me to a gentle and compassionate grief counselor or medium, who can support me in healing from the loss of my departed loved one/s. Thank you for reminding me that my loved one's are always with me in spirit and for helping me to connect with them as well.

~Appendix~
<u>Meditations</u>

Archangel Raguel

Thank you for leading me to new friends, relationships, and people who are aligned with my own natural interests and passions. Thank you so much for helping me to be introduced to people of high integrity, compassion, honesty, and love. Thank you for supporting me in creating lasting positive relationships and to also release the relationships which are no longer serving me. I know that as I continue to move forward upon my path, that my relationships will shift and change. Thank you for guiding me throughout these shifts and changes, all along the way.

Archangel Zadkiel

Thank you so much for helping me with my school work, studies, and understanding and retention of new information, material, and ideas. Thank you for supporting me in all of my learning and teaching endeavors. Thank you for continuing to open me up to my thirst for knowledge and also ways to support others in their joy of learning as well.

Archangel Chamuel

Thank you so much for helping me to find what it is that I am seeking in all areas of my life. Knowing that in truth I have what I am seeking already sitting inside of me. I appreciate your support in gently leading me by the hand to the people, places, and opportunities that I would like to find and experience within my life. I know that all I need to do is ask and you will be with me helping me to find what it is that I want or need.

~Appendix~
<u>Meditations</u>

Archangel Uriel

Thank you so much for holding your beautiful lamp of light and peace as you help to lead me to the next places and phases of my life. I know that I am fully supported as I continue to move forward upon my path; and I thank you for being a bright light upon that path. Thank you for illuminating all that I am and all that is available to me now, and always.

Archangel Nathaniel

Thank you for supporting me in getting out of my own way and to begin to move forward upon my path today. Thank you for supporting me in taking guided action in making positive and much needed changes within my own life. I know that I have all that I need to experience the life that I want; and I appreciate your support and guidance as I make these much needed changes.

About The Author

Kristy M. Ayala, M.A. is an Author, Professional Speaker, and Intuitive Counselor. With both her Master's and Bachelor's degrees in Psychology, Kristy uses her professional and educational background in psychology in conjunction with her spiritual gifts to best support her clients. Kristy has been providing advising and support services to clients for over a decade; and enjoys being able to fully support people as they move forward on their path. Kristy enjoys helping people to achieve their goals and dreams by offering them guidance, information, and the ability to see their own potential.

Kristy's personal style is positive, compassionate, and powerful. While working with Kristy, you can easily feel her dedication and integrity in all that she does. Kristy believes in providing a balanced support system when working with clients which includes body, mind, and spirit. This in combination with her Master's and Bachelor's degrees in Psychology allow Kristy to offer a multifaceted support system to each of her clients.

Kristy is a Professional Life Coach, Angel Therapy Practitioner® Certified by Doreen Virtue, Ph.D., Reiki Master Teacher, Certified Clairvoyant Medium, and Certified Yoga Instructor. As a professional speaker, Kristy also teaches courses on a variety of spiritual and well being topics to students in the U.S. and abroad.

Kristy has worked as a University Faculty Member, Non-profit Director, University Academic Advisor, Family Law Mediator, Counselor, and Author. Kristy has published work that focuses on Angels, Archangels, The Divine Feminine, Health, Wellness, and Life Satisfaction.

Kristy's book *Angels Among Us: Messages from the Archangels* is available now.

Kristy's work has been published in *The Miracles of Archangel Gabriel*, *Mermaids 101*, *Mary, Queen of Angels*, *Archangels 101*, and *The Healing Miracles of Archangel Raphael* by Doreen Virtue, Ph.D., *Lotus Guide*, *A Next Step*, and *The Goddess Guide Online*.

You can connect with Kristy during her weekly radio show *Kristy's Connection to the Soul* on Blogtalk Radio. Kristy has been a guest on Hay House Radio, F.M. Radio, Blogtalk Radio, and Souls Journey Radio.

You can find more information about Kristy by visiting her website, www.kristymayala.com.

~Notes~

~Notes~

~Notes~

www.ingramcontent.com/pod-product-compliance
Lightning Source LLC
Chambersburg PA
CBHW020942100426
42741CB00006BA/618